Random Feelings
Aimed Words

Brian Layden Garrison

India | USA | UK

Dedication

to my Family and Friends

and the Few who are Both

Acknowledgments

I would like to thank my friend, Raquel, for believing that I could, and should, write this pamphlet of poetry.

Preface

This collection of poems explores the tension between self-doubt, cynical views of the world, and fleeting moments of hope. Through metaphors and introspection, I reflect on the complexities of love, attraction, and the struggle to find belonging in a chaotic world. These poems speak to the vulnerability of facing personal and societal challenges, while still seeking connection and optimism.

This work is for anyone who has felt out of place or struggled with self-worth, yet continues to search for meaning, however small. I offer these words as a reflection of my own journey, hoping they resonate with yours.

The Longing Day

The Longing Day is ahead
It appears ominous with only an eyelash
peeking around the corner
A circuitous grin protected by the shield of
hesitating development

My back of fledgling clarity presses firmly
Against the connecting wall of an inhabited
no man's land
Breaths dancing like the sporadic
worshipping the infrequent

It awaits the face-to-face masking of
seemingly abhorrent recognition
The realization to be pushed down beyond
the fires of a pitted lower intestine
"You Lose," remarks the Longing Day, "You
Lose Again"

My eyes turn the corner and face its hollow
and translucent grasp
No more than the weight of a forgotten
mentor's lecturing oblivion

"Healing Begins Now," remarks MY
Conscious
"Healing Begins Now and Forever"

Tomorrow?

A Belligerent dawn is upon us
The lips of the intolerant grow like a fungus
Dastardly and beset
Devoid of consent
The tide is rising from the hangnail moon
Fate is wallowing in a leather-bound dune
Forward and on to never contort our necks
Leaving the past and the future married in
sanctimonious wrecks
Will it be a circuit-bound consciousness?
Or a fiery baptism upon us?
Do better today
For tomorrow may wander astray

idka

Defining the inners of broken glass feelings
Sand derived from an eroded island
Each crashing wave wipes clean a
remembrance
The cold desolate breeze of a storm
Forever on the horizon clouds form and
lighting strikes
The pieces too fragmented
The sand too fine
Too coarse
Too hidden
Much of which never to be compacted,
portrayed, and displayed again
Are these grains worth finding?
The glass worth mending?
My offer worth accepting?
The confusion stings of an ebbing tidal hope
A feeling matched only by the boundless deep
And the knowledge of her

Her

Her hair, an auburn flowery pasture, acutely
unaware of just how perfectly it lays
Skin fair with a cream-colored array of
faultlessness
A heart stops
A hope restored
The storms amass no more behind her
radiance
Eyes of impossible brown and the forever is
encompassed in a moment of connection
A heart leaps again
Sly sophistication and warm benevolence are
released from lips so gentle and sympathetic
"Why was I not told of this celestial beauty
before?"
"Because you never would have believed me."
The lifeline of aspiration was thrown by the
hand
That must have awed in the one true
masterpiece of its design
That smile and that laugh and those
rosiness-suffused clouds form upon her face

Vanilla-scented aromatic at ease calms the
world around me and fills my senses
With windless whispers of peace
The light of my soul was always too clever to
be wholly engulfed by the dark
And Now
My Soul
The Light
They Emerge
In The Proximity Of
Her

Onlys and Beyonds

My life was filled with onlys and justs
A culmination of frayed flags being pushed by
the winds in the direction of an eclipsing
downward gaze
A hole built to be a suitcase for the exiled
destination
A claw was left behind as the only payment to
be passed along
My ruination then became lined with the
knives and the spoons alike
To unsheathe the swords from my ears and
release the guns from my eyes
To exemplify the possibilities that could be
obtained by detaching my hands
To believe the rhetoric of the knight and his
steed
My life now filled with myriads and beyonds

Honestly

And now
For some
Honestly, I'm tired of thinking about her
About all of the hers
The blonde, the brunette, and the auburn
The past, the present, and the never will be
The failed, the practical, and the fantasy
I'm ready to relinquish control
Oh yeah, I forgot
Honestly, I never had control
My thoughts conduct the aimless cadenza
I'm just a bystander to its untamed
performance
Fighting to get in edgewise
There aren't enough distractions in the world
Wait, there's another distraction
Maybe that one will help
...
Wonder what her name is?

Gray Fire

It's all gray fire
The smoke consumes the wounds
Tranquility now ablaze with malignant fumes
Cogent restlessness steadies wilder
My guardian angel is a charlatan and a liar
The soul's weighted pit commands the
darkness and looms
Refocused eyes glimpsing day again, the heavy
cloud always intrudes
Dissecting hope until bridges burned and
situations dire
It's coming to a point again and again and
again and again
There's no way but to secede from hope and
to extol the doubt
Familiar sinking, lost focus, nothing in front
now
The gray fire fueled by love's drought
Death greets me and asks only, "How?"

The Whites of Their Eyes

The whites of their eyes are much too small a
target
Aiming for the mirrored expression of a
congenial contortion
Hoping the second reveals a bond between
our yielded lives

Messages though bemused and intent
misconstrued
Bridges hammered together with nails of
open flame
And an analyzing peer of an otherwise
trembling fear

Their hearts travel to the cascading North
While the envoy forages in the subduing East
The covenant lost to the shadowy nebulous of
a ceaseless forest

A castle crumbles
For none to remember
Like dried twigs of a dam swept away in a
flood

All this I saw
All for a second
All when I aimed for the whites of their eyes

The Same

The darkness overcomes when the happiness
has fled
No love, No riches, No fulfillment can aid the
faltering serenity
The shadow is all
The nothing is all
It's getting late
Hopes wisp away, gusts of momentary relief
become shuddering chills
Flames fan, lingering a steady grasp forged in
solid-steel rage
When the happiness has fled, the darkness
overcomes
Nowhere to go but deeper down
It's much too late
No hatred
No resentment
Just constant affliction and an exertion of
apathy
The sky crumbles around, the horizon a cage
of empty solitude
It's forever too late
It overcomes

It has fled
It's one in the same

In the Belly

Swallowed through the gaps of clenching
teeth
The whale now becomes the new habitation
Sacrificial intent became a self-destructive
amend
A selfless gesture or an act of self-seeking jest?
Entrapment is ubiquitous
Lashing out from too much peering in
Years of numbing stagnant elation
Discovery in the stomach revealed a gift
An atlas appeared with a destination marked
X
Y next to it in a language only recently
recollected
Crawling upwards with half-hollowed nails
Wood from the predecessors' steps founded a
path
Stomping on the lips as a new pattern
Eye to eye and a nodding approval
Submerging down and diving again
The last of it steady, as it wasn't a fluke

Where Does it Go?

Where does the road fall to when it suddenly
drops off?
Does the navigator drop off with it?
Are they heading to an impossible future of
which I can't possibly fathom?
Should they be pursuing a destined path?
Or just follow a conveyor belt of quotidian?
Will they let me see their open future?
Would they obscure that sight with a flash of
indifference?
Are we not established by the same thread?
Could the needle ever tear through the
pinholes of our blankets?
Where does the road lead when the distance
has swallowed it?
Is the point a beginning or an end?
Will I ever get there?

The Default

I still see them with every passing gust of
boreal breath
I turn inward for a forever, for an answer to a
nothingness I have created

It embalms the vortex of the expertise
compiled by experience
It never being far from the fault line that is
the new predictability

The reasons to me are fashioned by backs
turned
The heir apparent to the misunderstanding of
credulous deeds

Not to be outdone by incandescent intestines
Not ready to re-ravel the appropriate synapse

Explore the alleviating softness that once was
offered
Embrace the warmth when you were truly left
out in the cold

Recall the last time you thought it to all crash
down
Recount that it never did
Did it?

It Happened Again

I'm feeling obsessive and I can't shake the
threat
It's becoming oppressive and I'm caught in the
net
The logic reassures but no ears heed the facts
My stomach still burns and there are knots in
my back
Scenarios run wild, dancing frantically bright
They're laughing with guile-ogling judgment
alike
Reassuring the doubts you know all to be true
They've spotted your weakness with those few
subtle clues
You thought they were different, thought
they'd share what you lack
But they found you extrinsic after you'd given
up your back
This happening time and again yet the pit
heavies anew
Your steps quieted them, your eyes held
justtttt a bit too
On to the next group to share in the plight

Yet you've already seen the ending in their
criticizing delight

Going Home

I don't want it
Any of it anymore
Purging my life
One benign catastrophe at a time
It is the new norm
No hiding from it
To jump, pull, or swing?
The only decision
My head feels tight
A band wrapped inside my skull
Like a crown of crystalized reflection
I see all the shadows of past, present, and
future
The plight scattered across a welcome mat
Doors are shutting one by one
Windows less visible than previously thought
possible
The hood now draped over
Goes on and on
Never stopping
Only bewildering
Just an act of going home... yeah, that's all it is

Autumn Leaf on the 5th of December

When is a goodbye the right time to slam the
front window?
Never again to peer through the dirty panes
Tilted downwards toward the autumn-tinted
flowing leaves
The scent only to linger in pausing moments
of a scorched remembrance
Second to only the wave of butterflies
dropping abruptly below the solar plexiglass
Faded streaks of rain to fill in the gaps of a
mind hoping
Dots drawn together to adhere to the
happiness that they deserve
Lights in the distance of a grassy hill and a
sharpened cloud's edge
Gleamingly reflecting backward as the
butterflies divebomb again
Meteors that burned up in a sky within the
reach of a fingernail
Impacts still cratered in an all too tender
layer of misshapen notions

Turning away to resurrected ghosts one last
time
Hardening the armor as it was always meant
to be
Forgetting that the window shattered well
before eyeing that one autumn leaf

Sedentary

In a cage, he sits
He waits
He looks out to a clear blue sky and it stops
There is nothing
Tree limbs perform in a rhythm conducted by
the wind
Birds chirp as their choir
Squirrels dance as their audience
A breeze hits his face for the first time in ages
Green turns to orange
Orange turns to brown
Brown turns to black
Sunlight embraces a single fistful of land
It is blinding
The day is beautiful
Yet still there is nothing
He returns to the comfortability of the dark
Waiting for it to turn into forever

Returns On-Demand

They have risen to take back what is theirs
Presenting themselves before me as a swaying
and seething throng
Surrounding in a sickle-shaped ensemble

My hand and my face and my back have
reinvented their inferno
The white indents open anew
Red again flows from a prior judgment

Jaws opened with eyes closed
Hands out with palms pointing to the
vulture's sanctum
Ears connected from the bottom of their
torsos to the points of their brows

I can taste the coterie and feel the buzzing
proposal
They demand the one offering I can salvage
An emptied tongue before them lays
glistening in a moon-lit amphorae

The Hideous Side

The Rage is wielded towards the entirety of
the congregation
It hangs from the point of an eroded and
frightened blade
Building and brewing
Lingering and evolving
Always new souls to be cast down by hope's
blinded white flag
New situations to reinforce the blade's layered
and folded steel
The folds are painful
The layers are heavy
Begging to be left aside
Freed to garnish the mists of its own needed
sorrow
It doesn't enjoy the fiery milieu any more
than the beholder
In a worn-out plea, it too requires rest
A needed release is all it implores

No Use to Be Found

Born in a place of useless grounding
All between the bustling lights of quick
thinking
And the steady pace of hard living

Comfortability sought in excess
All besides the echoing walls of burrowed
distress
The cohabitants competing for the hard lines
carved by their mowing progress

Souls stagnate into lust and dreams mulled
over into dust
All while the fingers point upward toward the
cracked pavement
Shooting from their mouths of day's past
enlightenment

Stuck like the action of a swinging golden
plate
All moving to skirt around the forward
leaning gate

Realizing that nativity was an all too common
mistake

Forward Momentum

Few memories may
Last in a perfect balance
To keep the soul whole

Never look behind
Seek slowly the future truths
Look now, look forward

Engulf the current
Break through statues of regret
Rejoice in the now

Five Equals What?

Everything edited through the five points of
interlacing discovery
A constant truth is accepted, although a chain
may be broken in route
Distortion could have crept in through the
gap between soil and flesh
Faint drafts of snakeskin-entangled chimes
Together they amounted to a hooked
covenant
Slipped through the amassing stardom and
laid rest to a previously accepted solace
Believing to encounter the plugged holes of a
sunken ship
Realization appears through cracks of light
A rosy fumigation crossed the palatable stock
of relished requests
Two holes drilled in and mushroomed out
Two horizontal wounds
Finally lacerated again

The Second

For a second elates with a prospect
Completely devoid of pain and suffering
All is harmonized and tranquil
Everyone has an instant of conclusive content
Eyes fill the spaces between with the meekest
of gavels

Hands reached out and folded around
One after the other after the other after the
other
Like furrows of dreams seeded by unifying
tears
A beauty never before kindled
And a love never to be shared again

In an instant, a million-year debt was atoned
Sorry filled the winds with bowed heads
Ratification thundered through the trees the
mountains the oceans the deserts and the
skies
For a second was allied by the only similarity
we all have left
That the next million years need to be

swaddled and adorned

A Look

That disgusting twisted vulgar look
It's a brief glimpse behind the curtain of what
a clay-footed man has to offer
The shield slipped from the wretched and
decayed immaterial center
Although a shield may invoke a resemblance
of honor
A notion far too gone from the crevasses that
enter through sockets and end between
ribs
Fodder is laid out before the branches as a
shadowy cracked door
Inherited by roots that grew from the
superiority only men trip over
Apples fall to roll and hide the marred cores
they couldn't run from
Reigning narratives spew out all over the field
of plastic blades
Picked up by the hawks hunting
fruit-fattened worms
Beastial accounts of savage cogs rotate in piles
As flesh catches sudden gusts of
miscellaneous gales

Barren sods soiled with inward remains of
once-hidden sin
No eyes left now to gaze upon the disfigured
slip of a well-envisaged disguise

What Reaction Did You Expect?

Share what you hold dear
But beware the uniformed leer
For that which you share ceases to mirror you
soul
The burning reflection conjoins with the cold
Give away what you love until it's withered
and beaten
Make a plate of your linings to be served and
eaten
Another bridge pillaged like a
shrink-wrapped toy
The indifference amounted as they murdered
your joy
Should have relinquished the same old
bequest
Normal straights and narrows for them not to
detest
They shove back your hands that hold the
things you adore
You put them back in your heart to be
heckled no more

Though they never fit again ever the same
Aren't you glad they listened, aren't you glad
they came?